WELCOME

AMAZING ACADEMY.
SPYING
SCHOOL OF
SPYING AND ESPIONAGE

This manual teaches you all you need to know to set forth on a career in espionage. It's packed with interesting facts and exciting information, all backed up by a practical hands-on book giving you exercises to try out for yourself. Along with this manual, your Amazing Academy pack should contain the following items:

HANDS-ON BOOK • ID CARD • CAMPUS MAP • SPY PEN • FAKE ID CARDS

PLEASE CHECK THAT ALL THESE ITEMS ARE PRESENT AND CORRECT BEFORE PROCEEDING. YOUR SURVIVAL AS A SPY MAY DEPEND ON IT! AND DON'T FORGET TO LOG ON TO WWW.AMAZING-ACADEMY.COM USING YOUR UNIQUE ID CARD.

READY TO GO? GOOD – START SPYING!

IMPORTANT NOTES FOR ALL STUDENTS
SPYING AND ESPIONAGE IS NOT EASY! WHILST MANY OF THE EXERCISES ARE HARMLESS, SOME OF THEM SHOULD BE TREATED WITH CAUTION. IF YOU WANDER AROUND SPYING ON STRANGERS YOU WILL GET INTO TROUBLE AND WORST OF ALL, BREAK YOUR COVER AS A SPY. WE'RE AWARE THAT NOT ALL OF OUR STUDENTS HAVE THE AMAZING ACADEMY TUTORS ON HAND TO ADVISE THEM. SO IF YOU ARE GOING TO TRY OUT SOME OF THE TIPS AND EXERCISES IN THIS COURSE, WE RECOMMEND THAT YOU APPOINT A PARENT AS A HOME TUTOR TO HELP YOU. THEY MIGHT LEARN SOMETHING AS WELL. WHEN YOU SEE THE HOME TUTOR SYMBOL, IT'S TIME TO GET THEIR HELP.

HOW IT WORKS

The course is broken into four sections. Each section has a number of lessons, often with an exercise or test for you to do. Successful completion of the test will gain you credits, which will go towards your final score. (You can keep a record of your credits in the hands-on book accompanying this manual.) All tasks are self-assessed, which means you mark yourself. Our staff are often sent away on missions, so they don't have time for that sort of thing.

SECTION 1: BASIC AND ADVANCED DECEPTION
Tutor in Deception and Disguise: Mme. LeFarge

This section covers disguise – the fine art of pretending to be someone else. You'll learn how to put together a wardrobe of disguise, what documents you need to create a false identity, and how to change your appearance in a hurry.

SECTION 2: APPLIED SURVEILLANCE
Tutor in Surveillance: Superintendent George Johnson

If you're a spy, you've got to learn how to spy on people. This section teaches you the observation skills you'll need in order to learn how to track people, and how to avoid being tracked yourself.

SECTION 3: CODES AND CIPHERS
Professor of Codes and Cryptology: QXTL3 GG569

Codes and ciphers are one of the most important tools of the spy's trade. In this section you'll learn how to create secret codes, use a cipher wheel and even make your own invisible ink.

SECTION 4: GADGETS AND EQUIPMENT
Tutor in Advanced Gadgetry: Prof. James Rimmington

Every spy needs their secret gadgets. Sometimes you need special weapons as well. In this section, you'll learn what gadgets are available and how to use them.

MEET THE TUTORS

DIRECTOR OF STUDIES:

Agent X

After a dazzling career in espionage, Agent X was appointed Director of Studies at the School of Spying in ▇▇▇▇▇ Before that he was ▇▇▇ and then ▇▇▇▇ Then he worked undercover in ▇▇▇▇, ▇▇▇▇ and New Jersey. His many awards for bravery include the ▇▇▇▇ the Silver ▇▇▇▇ and an enormous ▇▇▇▇ made of brass. His poodle Binky was also employed by MI6 and went on several covert operations, disguised as a cat.

- Age: ▇ years
- Height: ▇▇▇▇▇
- Weight: ▇▇▇▇
- Skills: Disguise, surveillance, unarmed combat

Agent X and Binky during a recent covert operation exercise. The ability to squeeze into tight spaces is useful for a spy. Binky's cat disguise is less convincing.

CLASSIFIED: TOP SECRET

MEMO

To: Agent X
From: Head of Covert Ops
Re: Future Plans

It is the right time for you to move on, I think. The Russians know now that you penetrated the nuclear bunker disguised as a wastepaper basket. We know they know, but as to whether they know that we know they know, well, I don't know. Either way, now that you have retired from field operations, I have talked to the P.M. about the idea of you writing a manual for new agents. He agrees that some kind of training for young spies would be ideal, but wonders if it wouldn't be better for you to start a proper training school. Somewhere where they can learn from you and other specialists. What do you think?

PROFILES

TUTOR IN DECEPTION AND DISGUISE:

Mme. LeFarge

Mme. Lefarge's skills in disguise are legendary. During the course of one famous evening in Vladivostok, she disguised herself as a Russian Dancer, a German Countess and, amazingly, a Greek Salad. She will advise students on how to disappear into the crowd, how to transform themselves into another person and where to get the best false documentation. "LeFarge", you will not be surprised to learn, is not her real name.

- Age: Not known
- Height: Haven't a clue
- Weight: Your guess is as good as mine
- Skills: Disguise, deception, acting, tax-avoidance, crochet

TUTOR IN SURVEILLANCE:

Superintendent George Johnson

Superintendent Johnson will show students how to follow suspects, and avoid being followed themselves. In all his years working with the police's crack surveillance teams, Superintendent Johnson only ever failed to see one thing. Unfortunately it was an open trap door. Following the accident, he retired to the Amazing Academy and now teaches students all the skills he has learnt.

- Age: 49 years
- Height: 1.82 m (5 ft 11 in)
- Weight: 89 kg (14 stone)
- Skills: Tracking, surveillance, needlepoint

TUTOR IN CODES AND CRYPTOLOGY:

QXTL3 GG569

GG569's skills in cryptology are so great that no-one has yet managed to work out what his real name is. He will be your tutor for all forms of codes and ciphers. A boy genius, when he was seven he invented the Securo-matic, a cipher-machine so fiendishly complicated that even the instruction manual needed a team to crack it. He has since established himself as one of the greatest code-makers the world has ever seen. Not bad for a 12 year old.

PROFILES

- Age: 12 years
- Height: 1.47 m (4 ft 10 in)
- Weight: 44 kg (7 stone)
- Skills: Codes, ciphers, gameboy

TUTOR IN ADVANCED GADGETRY:

Prof. James Rimmington

"R", as he is known, is an expert on all forms of weaponry and gadgets. He has supplied amazing gadgets for the intelligence services of Britain, USA, France and Germany. Sometimes all at once. He can often be seen at major arms fairs, wandering around the exhibits, ticking off all the ones that he invented.

- Age: 72 years
- Height: 1.44 m (4 ft 8 in)
- Weight: 63 kg (10 stone)
- Skills: Engineering, electronics, particle physics, and pastry-making

FINDING YOUR WAY AROUND

Finding your way around the Department is not easy, but then you are supposed to be spies after all. Please note that the caretaker regularly places booby-traps and alarms to test students. Anyone spotting these will gain credits. Anyone luring another student into them will gain double credits.

SECRET ENTRANCE FROM LIBRARY

The Department is entered via a secret entrance in the Amazing Academy Library. To find the entrance, go through the library to the reference section at the back. In the section on "Pets," you will find a book called *Keeping Poodles for Pleasure*. Pull the book towards you. The shelf will slide to one side, revealing a lift, which will take you down to the Spy School main entrance.

SURVEILLANCE DEPARTMENT

The Surveillance Department includes a range of tools and resources to help you keep tabs on other spies, students, etc. The department is wired to hidden cameras around the campus.

DISGUISE DEPARTMENT

As well as a fully stocked costume store, the Department has a workshop for forging documents and a fully trained wig-maker for that finishing touch.

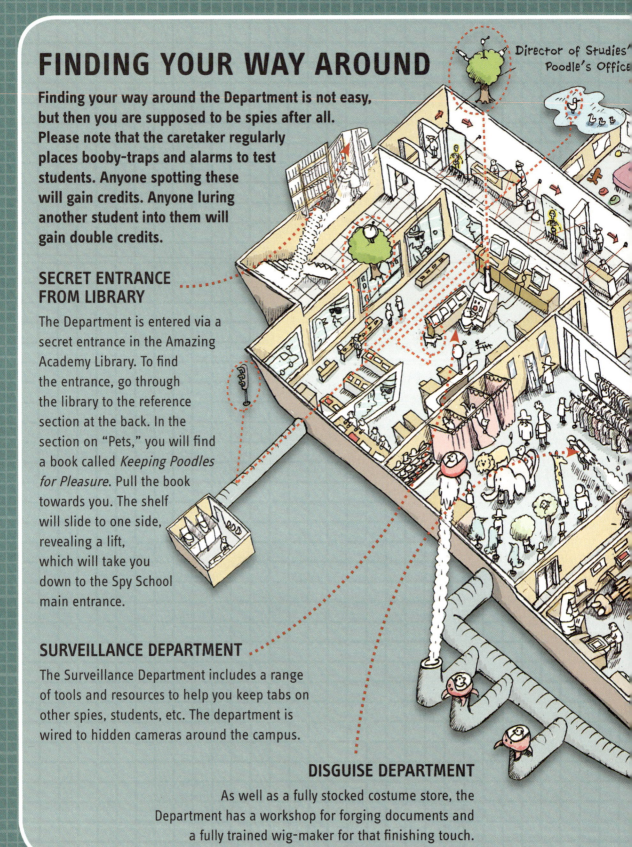

Director of Studies' Poodle's Office

SPY SHOP

The place to get all your gadgets and equipment. Everything from night goggles to fake passports; from micro-transmitters to voice analysers. We also sell a wide range of weapons, including guns, knives and poisoned blow-darts. Also dog biscuits for Binky.

Director of Studies' Office

These toilets double as an emergency exit. Flush three times and you'll emerge through the Academy duck pond.

THE CODE ROOM

Open daily. Codes changed each day. Using the latest coding devices – as well as those from historic times – the code room is where you learn to encrypt and decrypt messages. The door is opened by code (of course), which is changed daily. If you forget it, you will have to break in, although if you do break in, you'll earn extra credits.

Large, very complicated computer. Don't press any buttons.

EQUIPMENT AND COMBAT TRAINING AREA

This is where you will learn to use all your equipment; as well as how to defend yourself when your weapons run out of ammunition. (Or, for those of you who buy any weapons from Kipperbung, when your weapons invariably blow up the first time you use them.)

EQUIPMENT

EQUIPMENT CHECKLIST

This course will teach you some of the skills you need to survive in the murky world of spying and espionage; the intelligence you need to gather intelligence. But along with quick wits and brain power, you'll need some basic equipment; the tricks of a very tricky trade, as it were.

Here's what you could do with from the start:

- ☐ Miniature Camera
- ☐ Cash in dollars, pounds sterling and euros (real or forged)
- ☐ Miniature transmitter
- ☐ Code book
- ☐ Fake ID documents (see p.16)
- ☐ Rubber gloves (to prevent fingerprints)
- ☐ Secure channel mobile phone
- ☐ Maps

AGENT X SAYS, "MINIATURE CAMERAS ARE NOW SOMETIMES SUPERSEDED BY MOBILE PHONE CAMERAS. HOWEVER, SINCE EVERYONE KNOWS ABOUT MOBILE CAMERAS, THE CLEVER SPY MIGHT CHOOSE TO USE SOMETHING ELSE. YOU CAN GET MINIATURE DIGITAL CAMERAS THAT ARE DISGUISED AS PACKETS OF SWEETS, FOR EXAMPLE, OR WHICH LOOK LIKE WRISTWATCHES. YOU ARE ADVISED AGAINST BUYING THE KIPPERBUNG COVERT MINIATURE CAMERA, HOWEVER, SINCE, STUPIDLY, THEY HAVE JUST DISGUISED IT AS A BIGGER CAMERA.

BASIC AND ADVANCED DECEPTION

Bonjour, my little petits-pois!
I, Madame LeFarge, Mistress of Disguise, welcome you to this part of the course. I have spent many years learning the basics of being a spy. When you are a woman like me, you have to master many different subtle tricks; you cannot rely on brute force to get the job done. (Although I have a mean karate chop when I'm angry. And, I once knocked out three foreign agents using my handbag – which wasn't very surprising as it did have a brick in it.) In this section we will concentrate on deception: how to pretend to be someone else. We will also look at how you pass on information through drop points and other means of contact. So read on my little cabbages – and start deceiving your opponents!

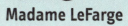

Madame LeFarge

IN THIS SECTION

1. IN THE BACKGROUND

2. WHAT ARE YOU DOING HERE?

3. DISGUISES

4. QUICK CHANGES

5. CREATING A FALSE IDENTITY

6. PASS IT ON . . .

BLENDING IN

IN THE BACKGROUND

The secret of disguise is to find something that blends in and makes you appear perfectly normal. You must remember, my little gherkins, that the job of a spy is <u>not</u> to get noticed. All those spies on film (those gorgeous good-looking men and women) would make useless agents because they would be too noticeable. They drive glamorous cars and wherever they go there are explosions and fights. No, no, no, our aim, my petits carrots, is to blend in with our surroundings.

This is not just about clothing, it's about the job you do and the role you play. So many of the great spies have been truly unremarkable people to look at: small, dull, a little boring even. As a spy, you want people to forget they have ever seen you. That is why the best spy ever will never be known. Because he, or she, will never be discovered.

In general, DO NOT:

- wear brightly coloured clothes – especially very loud, Hawaiian-style shirts
- dye your hair an unusual colour or have tattoos, etc.
- dress in smart or glamorous clothes (unless everyone else is wearing them)
- walk with a limp
- speak loudly or make wild gestures
- look directly at CCTV cameras – you should look at the ground or read a magazine instead
- order fancy food or drinks – you should order simple food, nothing unusual. Waiters may not remember someone who ordered the spaghetti bolognaise; but someone who ordered the Chef's Special Spit Roast Pig is noticeable. And drink beer. Not fancy martinis made in highly unusual ways.

AGENT X SAYS, "THE REAL LIFE OF A SPY IS NOT THE GLAMOROUS LIFE PORTRAYED IN THE FILMS. THE TRUTH IS THAT YOU WILL LIVE IN THE SHADOWS, AWAY FROM THE LIMELIGHT. YOUR FAMILY AND FRIENDS WILL NEVER KNOW THE REAL JOB YOU DO. EVEN FELLOW STUDENTS ON OTHER COURSES HERE AT THE AMAZING ACADEMY SHOULD NOT BE TOLD THE DETAILS OF YOUR COURSE."

"MY WIFE, FOR EXAMPLE, THINKS THAT I AM A LIBRARIAN. WHEN I HAVE TO GO ON MISSIONS OVERSEAS, I TELL HER THAT I AM VISITING THE INTERNATIONAL LIBRARIANS' CONVENTION. THE OTHER DAY SHE FOUND A STUN GUN IN MY LUGGAGE; I JUST PERSUADED HER THAT MY LIBRARY WAS TAKING A VERY TOUGH LINE ON OVERDUE BOOKS."

WHAT ARE YOU DOING HERE?

All spies should cultivate the art of "fading into the background" but that doesn't always mean you have to wear dull or drab clothing. It means that you aim to avoid raising any suspicion about your presence. The most important thing for a secret agent is to have a good reason for being somewhere. People will not ask questions if they think it is perfectly natural to find you there.

A clown outfit, for example, would be a stupid thing to wear to a funeral – but perfectly natural to wear in a circus. If you were trying to infiltrate a school or college, you would try to wear the right uniform. So, my little pommes frites, think first about the place you are going and the people you are trying to spy on. What uniform or clothing would be normal for them? What kind of person would "fade into the background?" There are many spies in this street scene. One of them, however, has badly misjudged his choice of disguise.

BLENDING IN

EXERCISE 1.1:
"RIGHT UNIFORM" HANDS-ON BOOK P.2
CREDITS: UP TO 10

DISGUISES

We have already discussed the idea of blending in with the background. So when it comes to a disguise, do not rush for the dressing up box. If you go out into the crowd looking like a cowboy, you will probably be noticed (unless you're herding cattle or attending a rodeo, of course, in which case, don't wear a suit).
The good news is that you can easily disguise yourself in different ways, without having to resort to fancy dress. A good spy will have a range of simple clothing that he or she can mix and match to change their appearance.

GLASSES

Few things alter your appearance as quickly and easily. Try to collect a range of glasses, either sunglasses, or old reading glasses (you can sometimes find these at charity shops, flea markets or jumble sales). Take out the lenses, otherwise you'll end up bumping into everything.

COATS AND JACKETS

An old coat can have padding sewn into it to make you appear larger than you actually are. You can also buy lightweight reversible jackets – these are jackets which can be worn "inside out" so that the lining turns into the outside.

HATS

Get yourself a wide range of hats. Beanie hats, baseball caps, fedoras, etc. Just make sure you match the hat to the rest of the clothing. A person dressed as a businessman but wearing a baseball cap looks a bit strange! Headscarves can also offer a quick and simple way to change your appearance.

OVERALLS

These are useful for disguising yourself as a workman. They can be put on quickly (see p.14) and they act as a kind of "uniform". Put a Velcro patch on your overalls and you can stick on different company badges. That way you can use the same set of overalls to work for the post office, the phone company or the road repairers, just by swapping the label around!

AGENT X SAYS, "THE IMPORTANCE OF GETTING THE RIGHT DISGUISE CANNOT BE STRESSED TOO HIGHLY. ON MY LAST MISSION, I GOT A BIT MUDDLED AND, INSTEAD OF A BUILDER'S UNIFORM, ARRIVED AT THE CONSTRUCTION SITE OF AN ENEMY ROCKET BASE DRESSED AS A PIRATE (COMPLETE WITH PARROT). I HAD TO PRETEND THAT I'D COME STRAIGHT FROM MY SHIP AT THE DOCKS. FORTUNATELY I WAS STILL ABLE TO OBTAIN THE PLANS FOR THE BASE, HIDE THEM AND MAKE MY ESCAPE."

DISGUISES

DISGUISE ESSENTIALS

Use Velcro to stick different badges on the overalls. That way you can work for different organisations.

Different glasses can instantly transform your appearance.

A lot of padding in a jacket will make you look bigger than you are.

Make sure you wear the right hat with the right outfit.

Overalls will give you an official appearance.

EXERCISE 1.2
"SPY WARDROBE"
HANDS-ON BOOK P.3
CREDITS: 10

QUICK CHANGES

Here are some of my favourite quick ways to change your appearance:

- Start with more and go to less. In other words, start with a coat and a hat, then, if you have to make a quick change, take the hat and the coat off and stow them in a bag.
- Use a reversible jacket; that's a jacket that you can wear inside out. Just nip into a toilet, or down an alleyway, reverse the jacket and you'll come out looking totally different.
- Use overalls. We have already seen that these are useful and the good thing is they cover your clothes.

These diagrams show how quickly you can change, if you have the right clothing.

EXERCISE 1.3
"QUICK CHANGE"
HANDS-ON BOOK P.4
CREDITS: 15

QUICK CHANGES

CHANGING YOUR HAIR

A good way to disguise your appearance is to change your hair. If you have long hair this works really well. But, my little turnips, if you are bald, it gets a bit tricky. But then you could always wear a wig. (I have always been blessed with long hair, which I could fashion in any manner. If things got particularly desperate I could simply comb it all over my face and pretend I was a hearth rug.)

Here are some things you can do:

1. Brush your hair back and gel it down.
2. Part your hair to one side or the other.
3. Use hair straighteners to straighten wavy hair.
4. Dye your hair a different colour.
5. Put your hair up in a bun or knot.
6. If you have long hair you can tuck it all up under a tight-fitting cap.

WIGS

One of the best ways to disguise yourself (particularly for girls) is to wear a wig. However, you need to make sure that the wig is a good wig. A poor, ill-fitting wig, will only draw attention to yourself. For this reason, I always advise spies not to bother with fake moustaches and beards, etc. Because unless they are professionally done, you always end up looking like . . . well, like someone wearing a fake beard, actually.

CLASSIFIED:
TOP SECRET

MEMOSKI
Classified: Topski Secret.
To: Head of Kaftanistan Secret Service
From: Berlin Office
Re: Break In by Hairy Man

Honoured Comrade, you must know that the Berlin Office has had a security breach last night when we were off celebrating Glorious Leader's Monthly Birthday. It appears that the secret datafile containing the Glorious Leader's Plans for World Domination has been stolen. The culprit, as you can see from the CCTV picture, was a man with a very large head of hair. Indeed, one of our Alert Guards of the Republic said, "It looked like he was wearing a poodle on his head." Needless to say, we have been hitting each other all morning as punishment. I look forward to being further punished, possibly by sending to very cold Siberian Office. In meantime, we do all we can to trace hairy intruder with hair that barks.

EACH PLAY (U) 12345678   12:34:45

CREATING A FALSE IDENTITY

Ultimately a good disguise is not necessarily about clothes. Nowadays people argue that what you wear matters less than what you carry – in terms of documentation. Successful businessmen, for example, used to wear expensive suits. Nowadays they're just as likely to be dressed in a T-shirt and jeans. What matters is the identity cards they carry – their passports, credit cards, driving licences, etc. So make sure that you don't rely on just clothing alone. Get all the other little things. Creating a cover is about attention to detail.

HERE ARE SOME ITEMS OF IDENTITY THAT YOU MIGHT FIND USEFUL TO HAVE:

PASSPORT

Vital for crossing borders. These are expensive and difficult to obtain. When you leave the Academy and start working for a proper spy organisation, they will help you. (For the advanced student, they are available from the Amazing Academy Spy Shop. The most important thing is to use a passport from a country that is at peace with the country you are visiting. A Swiss passport is good, because Switzerland is a neutral country. Sweden is also good. You should also make sure that your costume and appearance matches the country. Don't use a Japanese passport unless you look Japanese; you will only excite suspicion.

BUSINESS CARDS

These are simple and easy to produce, and surprisingly effective. Business cards usually have the title of the business, your name (or your fake name) and the position you hold in the company. You can even collect them from real businesses and use them. Again, the trick is to produce the right business card for the job.

FAKE ID CARDS

These are more sophisticated than business cards, but a fake ID can work wonders. They are generally laminated or plastic credit card size cards, usually with your picture and a name on. They are harder to forge than business cards, but again, your organisation should be able to help you. You will find some fake ID cards in this pack. The Amazing Academy Spy Shop has a huge range of fake IDs, which you can order ready customised.

QUICK ON THE DRAW
Illustrator and designer
IVOR IDEA

Squark and Squeak
Specialist pet shop
BUD GEE
Parrot expert
45 Flamingo Avenue, East 14th Street, Trill,
67 123456 email:budgee@squarkandsqueak

HARD HATS
MASTER BUILDERS
BOB CONCRETE
Chief Jack Hammer Operator
33 Demolition Drive, Rubblestone,
email:bob@oohalovelycuppa

LETTERS, DIARY, PERSONAL ITEMS

Your aim is to create a believable identity. A good spy pays attention to details. So build up a picture of the person you are pretending to be. What do you do? Where do you live? What kind of family do you have? The more you can imagine about the character, the stronger your disguise will be.

Let's say you are pretending to come from Switzerland. Here are some little details that will add to the credibility of your disguise:

1. Some letters to your Swiss address. The letters should be in envelopes with Swiss stamps on. You can sometimes find postcards in charity shops – in this case you would try to find a Swiss postcard which you can personalise.

2. Get a diary and fill it with the details of your fake life: name, address, etc. Put in lots of fake appointments – use your imagination!

3. In your purse or wallet put some currency from the country you claim to come from (in this case some Swiss Francs. But you might also put in a few Euros as well).

4. See if you can find a photo of a family, perhaps some friends. Customise them with personal messages addressed to your false identity.

OBTAINING FALSE DOCUMENTS

The Amazing Academy Spy Shop has a range of identity documents for purchase. However, students are advised against purchasing Kipperbung's Latest World Passport Kit, as all the passports in it are based on designs last issued in 1895. Needless to say, anyone presenting a passport authorised by Queen Victoria is likely to be spotted.

AGENT X SAYS, "I CARRY A PILE OF OLD BUSINESS CARDS, WHICH CAN BE USED TO "PROVE" THAT I WORK IN TELEPHONE SALES, TEACHING, PUBLISHING, TRAVEL, ETC. THE ONLY PROBLEM I HAD WAS WHEN I GAVE SOMEONE A BUSINESS CARD THAT SAID THAT I WAS DORIS FILSOM, CHIEF EXECUTIVE OF THE DOGGYKLEEN CANINE CLEANERS. FORTUNATELY I WAS ABLE TO CLAIM THAT IT WAS A PRINTING ERROR, THAT MY REAL NAME WAS BORIS ELSOM AND THAT MR. BINKY WAS ONE OF MY CLIENTS."

DOGGYKLEEN
CANINE CLEANERS

DORIS FILSOM
Chief Executive

15 Dalmation Drive, Yorkie, YAP1 RUF
019 222 4356 email:doris@shinypaws

EXERCISE 1.4
"WHO ARE YOU?"
HANDS-ON BOOK P.5
CREDITS: 10

PASS IT ON . . .

Sooner or later, my little cabbages, you will have to pass on the information you have gathered. These may be enemy plans, pictures or code messages; all of which need to be passed on. But how will you do it? Mobile phones can be scanned and computers can be logged. You can't exchange your messages openly; you never know when you are being followed. What is needed is a way for you to pass information to your contact. You need to leave your messages in a place that you and your contact have agreed on. This is called a drop

PREPARING A MESSAGE FOR THE DROP

Put it in a pen

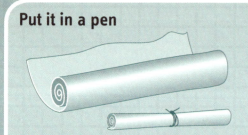

The easiest way is to write your message on a small piece of paper, roll it up, then tie it or tape it. This will form a small tube, which can be hidden inside an old pen or hollow twig.

Cover it with leaves

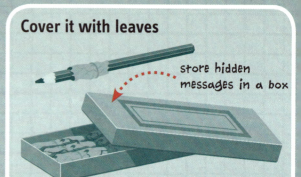

store hidden messages in a box

You can make a fake cover out of leaves, by wrapping a leaf around the message.

Creating a fake twig

This is a good hiding place for rolled-up messages. All you have to do is hollow out the soft interior of a twig so that it forms a kind of tube. Make sure your contact knows the hiding place otherwise they could end up hunting through a lot of twigs!

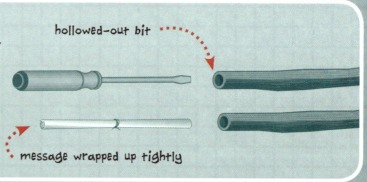

hollowed-out bit

message wrapped up tightly

DROP LOCATIONS

Spies normally have several drops in one location. To indicate which of the drops they have used, they leave a sign. Let's take a park as an example. The drop points may be in a hollow log, under a signpost, in a wastebin or under a particular stone.

What you do is this:

1. Go to the park. Walk round slowly, maybe eating a sandwich, or admiring the plants and flowers. If you have to bend down to make the drop, have a reason for doing so, like tying your shoelace.

2. When you get to the drop, leave your information there.

3. Mark the drop zone in some way. This might be with a chalk mark (use a dull colour so it won't stand out) or a strategically placed pebble. This is called a signpost – it tells the contact which drop you have used.

4. Walk away calmly. When the contact collects the information he or she should remove the signpost.

Drop Locations in a Park

A public park is an ideal place to "drop" information. Make sure that your contact knows where the drop zones are and that you have clearly marked which drop zone you have used.

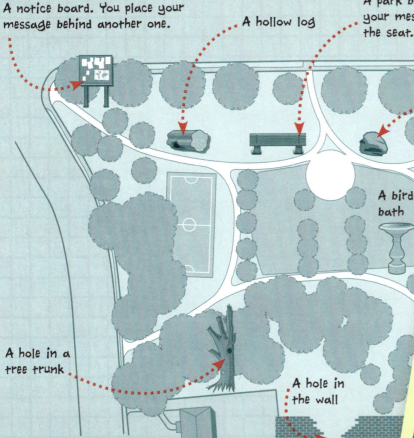

A notice board. You place your message behind another one.

A hollow log

A park bench. Pin your message under the seat.

A large stone

A bird bath

A hole in a tree trunk

A hole in the wall

AGENT X SAYS, "IF YOU USE DROP ZONES IN A PLACE LIKE A PARK, MAKE SURE THAT THE WILDLIFE DOESN'T GET INVOLVED. I ONCE HID SOME SECRET MICROFILM IN AN OLD, HOLLOW LOG, ONLY TO FIND THAT IT WAS THE HOME OF A HEDGEHOG, WHO, (THINKING IT WAS AN INSECT), ATE IT. MY CONTACT HAD TO TAKE THE HEDGEHOG HOME AND WAIT FOR THE PLANS TO EMERGE THE OTHER END, AS IT WERE. THIS WAS NOT PLEASANT FOR MY CONTACT. OR THE HEDGEHOG, COME TO THAT."

EXERCISE 1.5
"DROP IT!"
HANDS-ON BOOK P.6
CREDITS: UP TO 14

HIDING THINGS

Any spy has documents and information that it is necessary to keep hidden from prying eyes. Even information about the School of Spying and Espionage is to be kept hidden from students of other schools here at the Amazing Academy. So, where can you hide your secret messages? Here are some good places to try:

CREATING A HOLLOW COMPARTMENT IN AN OLD BOOK

 You will need an old book. Important: it should be one that is not used by – or even of interest to – anybody. So don't use a book that your friends or family might want to read. Instead, find one from an old bookstore with the most boring title you can imagine. Then, with the help of your home tutor, use a craft knife to cut out a section from the middle pages of the book. Use PVA glue to glue the pages lightly together. The result will be a container that looks like a book, but which is a great hiding place.

IN YOUR CLOTHING

Use tape to stick messages to the inside of a hat or behind a belt. You can get money belts – which look like ordinary belts but have a hidden pocket behind. Messages can be hidden in your shoes – under the inner sole, if you have one.

IN A BAG

Many bags have a lining on the base. You can hide secret messages, identity cards, etc. under the base.

AGENT X SAYS, "A GOOD AGENT WILL HAVE MANY SECRET HIDING PLACES, DESIGNED TO DEFEAT THE CLOSEST SCRUTINY. ONLY RECENTLY, AFTER INFILTRATING AN ENEMY ROCKET BASE, I HID THE SECRET PLANS TO AN ENEMY ROCKET INSTALLATION SOMEWHERE INCREDIBLY SAFE AND SECRET; A PLACE THAT NO-ONE WOULD POSSIBLY SUSPECT. THE ONLY PROBLEM IS THAT I CAN'T REMEMBER WHERE! SO IF ANY STUDENT FINDS THEM, THERE WILL BE A 50 CREDIT REWARD!"

MME. LEFARGE SAYS, "CONGRATULATIONS MY LITTLE MANGE-TOUT! YOU HAVE REACHED THE END OF THIS SECTION OF THE COURSE. MASTER THE ARTS OF DECEPTION AND DISGUISE AND YOU WILL BE WELL ON YOUR WAY TO BECOMING A MASTER SPY – LIKE ME!"

EXERCISE 1.6
"SECRET PLACES"
HANDS-ON BOOK P.7
CREDITS: 10

APPLIED SURVEILLANCE

Alright. Stand straight. A–TTENTION! This is where the real work starts. It's not all glamour being a spy, you know. And it's not all clever disguises and pretending to be someone else. A lot of the time it's simply following people around. Observing things is CRUCIAL to the spy's trade. We are trained to notice things. We are trained to follow people. We are trained to be nosy. That's where this section comes in. Here you will learn how to follow people – and how to avoid being followed yourself; to tail someone and how to shake off a tail (and no, I am not talking to you, Binky.) In this section we'll be looking at developing our observation skills. There are some gadgets that you can use to make the job easier. But mostly, it's just down to CONCENTRATION.
And, your own two feet.
So let's get MOVING!

George Johnson

Superintendent George Johnson

IN THIS SECTION

1. OBSERVATION SKILLS

2. SHADOWING A QUARRY

3. HOW TO MOVE SILENTLY

4. TRACKING OVER DIFFERENT TERRAIN

5. SPOTTING A TAIL

6. SURVEILLANCE KIT AND CLOTHING

7. EYES IN THE BACK OF YOUR HEAD

OBSERVATION SKILLS

As a spy, one of your key skills is the power of observation. How carefully do you you notice things? We are always looking around us, but how much do we ACTUALLY see? (For example, one of the sentences above is WRONG. Can you spot it?)* The fact is, we don't notice a lot. Observation requires DISCIPLINE and PRACTICE.

Here are some skills that ALL SPIES should master:

1. As you enter a room, notice where the exits are.
2. When you sit in a restaurant or cafe, sit with your back to the wall facing the door. Then you can see who comes in.
3. Make a mental note of the people in the room with you. Notice anything different about them?
4. Count. Count the number of people in the room, the number of cars in the car park, the number of waiters and waitresses. Practise, so you can do it fast and without using your fingers!
Remember: this is not a game. These skills could SAVE YOUR LIFE.

Look at the scene below: what would make you nervous as a spy? In your hands-on book there is a copy of the picture: mark the things that are suspicious.

*Answer: The second sentence has two "yous" in it.

EXERCISE 2.1
"FEELING NERVOUS?"
HANDS-ON BOOK P.10
CREDITS: LOADS!

SHADOWING A QUARRY

Shadowing is one of the basic tasks of a spy. Put simply, it means following someone and tracking their movements. The person who is doing the tracking is sometimes called a "tail"; the person who is being tracked is known as the "quarry". Of course, nowadays it is possible to track your quarry in a wide variety of ways; people can be tracked using satellite technology, car number plate recognition, or tracing the location of calls on mobile phones, for example. But for spies in the field, few things are as IMPORTANT as the ability simply to follow someone without them noticing.

HOW IS IT DONE?

Anyone can follow another person; the real trick is to follow someone, WITHOUT them noticing you. The good spy aims to follow his quarry through both town and countryside without being noticed. So, when you tail someone do not get too close to them. Do not stare fixedly at them, instead, CONCENTRATE on other things and glance at them from time to time.

STOP START

A common mistake by students is to walk behind the quarry, stopping and starting whenever the quarry stops and starts. If you mirror them this closely, they are BOUND to notice. Wouldn't you notice someone copying your every movement? The trick is to look as though you are NOT following them. If they stop, walk past them and then find an excuse to stop later so that they pass you again. You might spot something interesting in a shop window, for example, or stop to tie your shoelace, or pretend to send a text on your mobile phone.

RAPID CHANGE OF APPEARANCE

If you think you have been spotted, or if you just want to avoid such a thing happening, it might help to change your appearance quickly. While your quarry is stationary (e.g. in a cafe or library), find a secluded doorway. Using your rapid change wardrobe (see pp.14-15) you should be able to change your appearance.

Find a point when your quarry has stopped somewhere.

A few quick changes and your appearance is transformed.

HOW TO MOVE SILENTLY

There are times when you need to approach silently. You might be shadowing someone, you might be escaping, you might be breaking into a top-secret, government HQ (the last one is for ADVANCED STUDENTS ONLY).

SHADOWING

HOW TO MOVE WITHOUT BEING HEARD:

- First place the heel of your foot down, then slowly roll your foot towards your toes, onto the ground.
- Put each foot down flat then lift it up carefully.
- Breath quietly. Take long, slow breaths through your nose.
- Keep looking! Plan where you are going to plant your feet.

OTHER HELPFUL TIPS:

- Wear appropriate footwear. Large, heavy boots are no good. Wear soft-soled shoes.
- Avoid bare feet as these can stick on the floor.
- Step lightly. Do not stomp.
- When walking along a corridor, stay close to the walls, where the floorboards are less likely to creak. The same is true for staircases.
- Be sure your shoes fit. If they are too large for you, your feet will slide and it might produce a squeaking noise.
- Make sure your footwear is dry; wet shoes will squeak and damp footprints will give you away.
- Don't wear anything noisy! Don't wear chains, jewellery or keys that could jangle.

AGENT X SAYS, "ALWAYS REMEMBER TO TURN OFF ANY GADGETS THAT BEEP, BUZZ OR MAKE ANY OTHER NOISE. I REMEMBER A VERY STICKY MOMENT, JUST AFTER I'D STOLEN SOME TOP-SECRET MISSILE PLANS. I WAS CREEPING BACK THROUGH THE CORRIDOR, WHEN MY MOBILE PHONE WENT OFF. IT WAS MY WIFE, ASKING ME TO BUY SOME SAUSAGES FOR DINNER ON THE WAY BACK FROM "THE LIBRARY". FORTUNATELY, I WAS ABLE TO SWITCH OFF THE PHONE AND QUICKLY DISGUISE MYSELF AS A LARGE, POTTED PLANT, THUS AVOIDING DETECTION."

"ALTHOUGH BY THE TIME I'D EVADED THE GUARDS, ESCAPED THROUGH THE AIR-CONDITIONING DUCT, SLID DOWN A DRAINPIPE AND SCALED THE BARBED-WIRE FENCE, THE BUTCHERS WAS SHUT."

EXERCISE 2.2
"SILENT WALK"
HANDS-ON BOOK P.11 CREDITS: 25

TRACKING OVER DIFFERENT TERRAIN

When tracking suspects you have to take into account the types of terrain you will cross. Certain sorts of ground require different techniques – and there's some "noisy" ground (e.g. gravel, shingle, cornflakes) you would be better off avoiding altogether.

The important thing is not only to ensure that you are never seen, but also that the suspect does not see any signs that they have been followed. If they are in an open, secluded place and discover another set of footprints, they might just get suspicious.
So WATCH YOUR STEP.

How to tackle different terrains:

1. Walk on hard surfaces and keep to the hard part of the roads where possible.

2. Avoid stepping in mud or puddles.

3. If you have to cross a stream, use stepping stones. Or, take your socks and shoes off and go barefoot, replacing your shoes on the other side. That way you will avoid leaving damp footprints.

4. Stick to short grass where possible.

5. Do not tread in piles of sand or gravel. You might leave a trail behind you as you walk.

6. Leave gates and doors in the same position that you found them.

7. Do not walk through long grass, you will leave a trail.

8. Dead leaves are good for disguising tracks, but difficult to walk on quietly.

9. If you have to stop, keep in the shadows.

10. Try sliding your feet slightly as you walk, in order to blur the pattern left by the soles of your feet.

Be careful on stepping stones. People tend to notice someone shouting, "Aaargh!", followed by a splash.

GRASS

If you stop, keep in the shadows. It makes you harder to spot!

Make sure you remember to leave gates and doors as you found them.

HARD PAVEMENT

Avoid stepping in mud or puddles as you will leave a trail.

Dead leaves are good for disguising tracks, but they can be noisy.

DIFFERENT TERRAIN

Treading in piles of sand or gravel might leave a trail. Also, your shoes will need cleaning.

SAND

If in doubt, take cover!

LEAVES

Whatever you do, do not step on a duck.

AGENT X SAYS, "IF YOU HAVE TO CROSS MUDDY GROUND, OR SNOW, OR A BEACH – SOMEWHERE WHERE YOU CANNOT HELP BUT LEAVE A FOOTPRINT, TRY WALKING BACKWARDS. JUST REMEMBER TO LOOK BEHIND YOU. I ONCE WALKED BACKWARDS ACROSS A MUDDY FLOWER BED BUT FORGOT TO LOOK WHERE I WAS GOING AND FELL INTO A POND."

EXERCISE 2.3
"TERRAIN TRACKING" HANDS-ON BOOK P.12
CREDITS: 12

SPOTTING A TAIL

Sometimes YOU are the one being followed! Just remember that there will be people interested in YOU! It's all very well concentrating on following someone, but you must take steps to avoid being followed yourself.

HOW TO AVOID BEING TRACKED:

- Take precautions. Approach your destination by a roundabout route. If a tracker is waiting to pick you up, you will avoid him.
- If you go to the same destination a lot, vary your route each day – travel in different ways and at different times.
- Vary your speed. Do not walk fast the whole time. Walk fast and slow. If someone is on your tail, they'll have to vary their speed as well.
- Keep looking and listening for anything unusual. Is there anyone there who shouldn't be there? Is there a face that you recognise? Is there something out of place? Is there an unusually high number of CCTV cameras in the vicinity? Is anyone dressed as a clown?

CLASSIFIED: TOP SECRET

MEMOVITCH
Classified: Confidenski
To: Head of Kaftanistan Secret Service
From: Siberian Office
Re: Loss of Spy

Honoured Comrade, how my heart sang when I was given glorious task of following enemy spy. This would be chance to show Glorious Leader what I could do. Sad to say that despite using all my powers of cunning and stealth, enemy spy escaped. I picked him up walking his dog along October Revolution Street. Then he entered Cafe of A Thousand Calories. Then lost him! Only person coming out of Cafe was blind, old woman wearing unusually lumpy fur coat. Waited three hours but no sign of Enemy Spy. Needless to say I immediately punished myself by beating head against tree. I look forward to being further punished, possibly by sending to even colder Tibetan Office. In meantime we do all we can to trace blind, old woman with the wagging tail.

LOSING A TAIL

Hopefully, by taking these simple precautions, you will avoid being followed. But sometimes, you will notice that someone is, indeed, on your tail. So what do you do then? As we've seen, you can use your disguise skills to change your appearance (see pp.14-15). But here are some other tricks.

The direct approach

If you have spotted your tail, turn and walk directly towards him. He will either have to pass you and turn around, or, more likely, he will turn and walk in the opposite direction. While he is walking away from you, quickly turn round or disappear into a shop.

The sudden disappearance

Find a place with two or more possible "routes". They might be doors into different shops, or alleyways, or streets. Approach them from the opposite side of the road. Wait until the traffic builds up then cross as quickly (and safely) as you can. The aim is for you to be on one side of the street and your tracker on the other. Then, you simply wait for a large vehicle to come between you, like a bus or a lorry or tram. The moment that comes between you and the tracker, nip down one of the escape routes. When the vehicle clears you will have disappeared.

The dummy

- Go to the most crowded place you can find – train stations are good. Crowded supermarkets also offer lots of places to hide. It will be harder to tail you among crowds.
- Find a shop or public space with a number of entrances and exits. Enter slowly, and then, once inside quickly speed up towards the next exit. The person trailing you will not realise you have increased your speed and may be left behind.
- Go to the train station and get on a train. Then, just as it is about to leave, get off. Your tail will be left on the train.
- Find a shop or a public place with a lift. Get in the lift. If your shadow enters the same lift, exit just before the lift goes up. If he cannot exit in time he will be whisked away by the lift. If he does get out of the lift, he will make it obvious that he is following you. If he doesn't manage to get in the same lift as you, you can exit at the next floor and find a different way out of the building.

EXERCISE 2.4
"ESCAPE" HANDS-ON BOOK P.13
CREDITS: 10

SURVEILLANCE KIT AND CLOTHING

The secret of being a good surveillance operative is preparation. The more you are prepared to follow your quarry anywhere, the less likely you are to lose them. So get a basic tracking kit together and have it handy at all times. Then, whenever your quarry is on the move, you'll be able to follow them!

CLOTHING

- Remember, the aim is NOT to be seen. So wear ordinary clothes. It's best to wear drab, natural colours; greens and browns. That way if your quarry goes into the countryside, your clothes will blend in with the background.
- Do not wear shiny objects or jewellery. The sun can glint off them, attracting attention.
- Wear loose, easy-fitting clothes that you can run in, or use to take evasive action if necessary. Keep one or two accessories with you, so you can easily and quickly change your appearance (see pp.14-15)
- Wear soft-soled shoes so that you can walk quietly.
- It's a good idea to wear layers of clothing. That way, by taking a layer of clothing off, such as a jumper, you can change your appearance. However do not take your trousers off unless you have another layer underneath. People dressed just in their underwear are highly noticeable.

AGENT X SAYS, "ALWAYS TAKE THE CHANCE TO PRACTISE YOUR QUICK CHANGES. THE OTHER DAY, AFTER COMING BACK FROM MY MISSION AT THE ROCKET BASE, I WAS RETURNING MY PIRATE COSTUME TO THE SPY SCHOOL COSTUME AND DISGUISE STORE, SO I HAD A QUICK PRACTICE AT CHANGING MY APPEARANCE. ALTHOUGH I CAN'T IMAGINE WHY YOU'D EVER NEED TO – IT'S AMAZING HOW QUICKLY ONE CAN TRANSFORM FROM A PIRATE TO A WAITER."

EXERCISE 2.5
"TRACKING KIT"
HANDS-ON BOOK P.14
CREDITS: LOADS!

TRACKING KIT

If you are tracking a quarry, you're going to need some kit to help you. It helps to keep your hands free, so it's best to carry stuff in pockets if you can. If you have to take a bag, **MAKE SURE** that it's tight fitting and doesn't swing around. This is so it can't get caught on anything, should you have to track your quarry through bushes or undergrowth.

What you'll need:

- Notebook to record information, or jot down directions.
- Mobile phone. (Useful to alert your boss as to the quarry's whereabouts; you can also take pictures and play games if you're bored.)
- Compact binoculars. (Be discreet about using these. If you stand 6 m (20 ft) away, staring at someone through binoculars, they tend to notice.)
- Chalk, for leaving marks for fellow spies to follow. (Useful if the mobile phone stops working or you would be heard making a call.)
- Rations – high-energy bar. (Keep your energy up. You may not be able to stop and get anything to eat.)
- Mini-camera. (You can use a mobile phone, or a specialised spy camera.)
- Mini-torch. (Useful at night. Or if you suddenly need to hide in a cupboard.)

ELECTRONIC EQUIPMENT

Nowadays it is possible to track your quarry using a wide variety of electronic devices. You will find more on tracking devices in the "Gadgets and Equipment" section (see pp.50-55), but some you might consider using are:

- Miniature transmitter. This can be attached to the quarry's clothing or car, and sends signals back to base.
- Distance microphone. This allows you to "eavesdrop" on conversations happening a long distance away. However, they're big bits of kit so can probably only be used in woods, etc.

Both of these, of course, are expensive for individuals, but your spy agency may provide them for you.

TRACKING

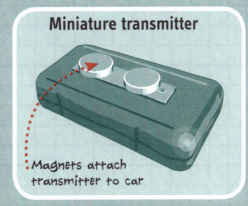

Miniature transmitter

Magnets attach transmitter to car

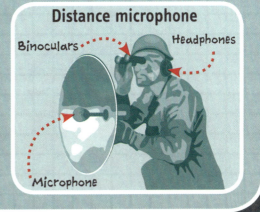

Distance microphone

Binoculars

Headphones

Microphone

LOOK BEHIND YOU

EYES IN THE BACK OF YOUR HEAD

One of the simplest covert devices is a pocket-book mirror. This allows you to sit at a cafe table, for example, and watch what is going on behind you.

POCKET-BOOK MIRROR

You will need:

- An old paperback book that you do not want anymore.
- Two small, make-up mirrors or mirror tiles.

Full instructions on how to make this mirror are in the hands-on book.

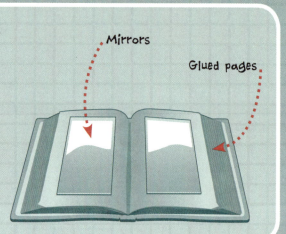

Mirrors

Glued pages

MIRRORED GLASSES

Other ways to see behind you are to view reflections in shop windows, or sit in a car and look through the rear view mirror. You can also buy special sunglasses with mirrors to each side, which allow you to look behind you.

Mirrored surface at edge of glasses

AGENT X SAYS, "WHEN PRACTISING YOUR SURVEILLANCE TECHNIQUES, IT'S BEST TO TRY THEM OUT ON FAMILY AND FRIENDS. SPYING ON STRANGERS MAY NOT GO DOWN TOO WELL!"

SUPERINTENDENT JOHNSON SAYS, "WELL DONE. IF YOU HAVE MADE IT THIS FAR, YOU HAVE PROVED YOURSELF TO BE A KEEN TRACKER. KEEP WORKING AT THESE SKILLS. KEEP YOUR DISCIPLINE AND KEEP CONCENTRATING. OH AND, KEEP USING CAPITAL LETTERS."

EXERCISE 2.6
"MIRROR BOOK"
HANDS-ON BOOK P.15
CREDITS: UP TO 15

CODES AND CIPHERS

Welcome. Or as we code experts say Xfmdpnf! (This is a very basic cipher. Can you crack it?)* This section of the spying course covers codes, ciphers, cryptograms and all manner of secret languages. We'll be looking at the different ways of getting your message across without it being intercepted or deciphered. And we'll explore the history of code-making; how secret services invented ways to send their secret messages in the past. We'll also be learning about other ways of sending secret messages, including hidden signals and even an easy-to-make invisible ink. For all you would-be spies out there, this is one of the most important sections of the course. So what are you waiting for? Let's get cracking!

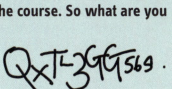

QXTL3 GG569

IN THIS SECTION

1. INTRODUCING CODES AND CIPHERS

2. LEARN TO SEND SECRET MESSAGES

3. LEARN TO USE CODES

4. LEARN TO USE A DICTIONARY CODE

5. A SIMPLE NUMBER CIPHER

6. MASTERING CIPHERS AND TRANSPOSITION CIPHERS

7. CRACKING CODES AND CIPHERS

8. MAKE YOUR OWN INVISIBLE INK

CODES AND CIPHERS

INTRODUCING CODES AND CIPHERS

It's all Greek to me . . .

Sending secret messages has a long history. In 480 BC the Persians planned to attack the Greeks. A Greek called Demaratus was living in exile in Persia and wanted to warn his fellow countrymen. Back then they didn't have pen and paper, they used wooden tablets covered with a layer of wax. So what Demaratus did was write his message on the wooden tablet itself, then cover it with a layer of wax. This allowed the information to be safely smuggled out of Persia. (The wax tablet was an easy solution; another way of smuggling a message out was to shave the head of a messenger, tattoo a message on there, then let the hair grow back to cover it before he went on his journey. All he had to do at the other end was get his head shaved and the message was revealed. This was not a good technique for urgent messages. Unless the messenger's hair grew really fast. From the Greeks, we also get the name for the science of sending concealed messages: "steganography", which is Greek for "concealed writing". Steganography, however, can only take you so far. If someone finds the hidden message (e.g. an enemy hairdresser), then all is revealed! So gradually agents began obscuring the message itself, writing it in code, so that, even if the message was discovered, it's meaning was hidden. This led to what is called "cryptography", which, surprise, surprise, is Greek for "hidden writing". Today, cryptography covers writing in codes and ciphers, which are two different things . . .

CODES AND CODE BOOKS

A "code" uses symbols or groups of letters to represent words or phrases. It is a kind of secret language. For example, you might use the phrase:

The porcupine will examine a skateboard in August.

And the actual meaning of this might be:

The ammunition will be dropped at midnight.

This is also called a "jargon code". These kind of codes were used in World War II, particularly when sending messages to resistance fighters over the radio. Obviously, to understand this you need a "code book" – a kind of dictionary showing what all the code words mean. Otherwise you might expect to see a porcupine on a skateboard when summer comes.

CIPHERS

A "cipher" is where each individual letter of a message is replaced by different letters or symbols, or where the letters are scrambled. This is known as "enciphering" (converting the message back to plain text is known as "deciphering"). To do this you need a cipher key. This tells you which letter has replaced which.

There are two kinds of ciphers: substitution ciphers and transposition ciphers. A "substitution cipher" changes the letters in the message to another set of letters. A "transposition cipher" shuffles the letters in the message around. "Encryption" covers both encoding and enciphering, while "decryption" covers both decoding and deciphering.

LET'S GO SUPER

So what if you combine both of these? What if you take a coded message and encipher it? Well, you've doubled the security and you've done something called " superencipherment".

BEING CRYPTIC

The science of creating codes and ciphers is known as "cryptography". The science of breaking codes and ciphers is known as "cryptanaylsis". Both of these together are known as "cryptology". The people who break codes are technically called "cryptanalysts" but that's just silly. Mainly, they're called "code breakers" (even though they might deal with codes and ciphers).

AGENT X SAYS, "THESE LONG WORDS ARE ALL VERY WELL, BUT THERE IS ONE SIMPLE FACT THAT YOU MUST ALWAYS BEAR IN MIND: WHATEVER YOU DO, KEEP YOUR CODE BOOK AND CIPHER KEY SAFE. IF AN ENEMY DISCOVERS YOUR CODE BOOK, THEN ALL YOUR COMMUNICATIONS ARE OPEN TO THEM. THE OTHER DAY, MY WIFE DISCOVERED OUR SPY SCHOOL CODE BOOK. I TOLD HER IT WAS A LIBRARY BOOK IN MEDIEVAL POLISH, BUT IMAGINE IF SHE WERE AN ENEMY SPY!"

"SO, ALL YOU TRAINEE SPIES: KEEP YOUR CODES SAFE. ANY STUDENT LOSING THEIR CODE BOOK WILL BE DOCKED 20 CREDITS. ANY STUDENT STEALING SOMEBODY ELSE'S CODE BOOK WILL GAIN 20 CREDITS. WE ARE SPIES AFTER ALL . . ."

EXERCISE 3.1
"CODE QUIZ"
HANDS-ON BOOK P.18. CREDITS: 14

LEARN TO SEND HIDDEN MESSAGES

**There are ways of writing hidden messages without encoding the words.
What you do is hide the message inside a lot of other stuff.**

USING A RULER

You will need a ruler and a piece of paper.

Here's what you do:

1. You lay a ruler across a piece of paper. Then you write out your message at regular intervals, say every 1 cm.

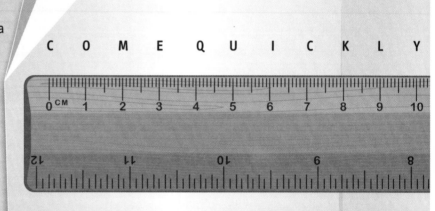

2. Take the ruler away and simply fill in the gaps with any other letters you can think of. You can make other words if you want to.

3. To read the message, your colleague simply needs to line a ruler along the bottom of the message and mark off the letters at 1 cm intervals.

SENDING A MASKED MESSAGE

This is a code that uses a cut-out "mask" to be read.

You will need two pieces of paper or card with "windows" cut out of them, like the example here.
You will keep one piece and the person you're sending your message to will have the other.

Here's what you do:

mask

> urgent
>
> meet me
>
> after
>
> class at the   railway
>
> station

This is not very urgent but if you were planning to meet me some time then we'll have to meet soon after August. I'm going to be attending class at the next town. I've bought a railway ticket at our nearest station but it means I can't come back for at least two months.

1. Get another piece of paper – the one you're going to write your message on. Lay your "mask" over the top of this. Write the message you want to send in the cut-out "windows" of your mask.

2. Remove the mask and fill up the gaps with other words.

3. When your contact gets the message, all he or she has to do is lay their mask over it and your real message will become obvious!

EXERCISE 3.2
"CREATE A CUT-OUT CODE"
HANDS-ON BOOK P.19 CREDITS: 10

LEARN TO USE CODES

JARGON CODE

A jargon code is where one word means another. For example, your code name might be AMBER, your Spy HQ might be WAREHOUSE. So, the message AMBER to WAREHOUSE is telling you to go to the HQ. Unless the enemy have your code book, this code is very hard to crack. To make a jargon code, you have to list all the words that you might use regularly, the meeting places, people you know, things you have to do. You could also have words to mean different times of day. Write them all down in a code book. Then, as long as your contact has the code book you will be able to send coded messages to them very easily.

AGENT X SAYS,
"MAKE SURE YOUR JARGON CODE WORDS ARE NOT OBVIOUS. FOR EXAMPLE, IF YOU USE "TUESDAY" AS A CODE WORD FOR "FRIDAY", OR "CENTRE" AS A CODE FOR "HQ". THEN THE MESSAGE "VISIT THE CENTRE ON TUESDAY", WHILE FACTUALLY WRONG, ISN'T VERY CRYPTIC. YOUR ENEMIES WOULD PUT A WATCH ON YOUR HQ. BUT IF YOU SAID, "VISIT THE HIPPO WITH A MELON" THEN IT'S MUCH MORE CONFUSING AND RAISES THE POSSIBILITY THAT YOUR ENEMIES WILL WASTE A LOT OF TIME LOOKING FOR SOMEONE TAKING LARGE PIECES OF FRUIT TO THE ZOO."

SYMBOL CIPHERS

We've seen that codes use words or symbols to replace whole words. Symbol ciphers use symbols to replace individual letters, One of the most famous of these is Morse Code, which uses dots and dashes for each letter and has been used in the military for many years. Although it's called Morse Code, it's actually a cipher, since each letter is replaced. Another well-known cipher is semaphore, which usually uses flags held in certain positions, but you can also write this out using the hands of a clock.

So, a message in semaphore might go:

A L L   S P I E S   T O   H Q

USING A PIGPEN

You can easily build your own symbol cipher by creating what is called a "pigpen"; that's a 3 x 3 box like this:

Then you write letters in groups of three, as shown in the example. Of course you don't have to put them in this order, you can put them in whatever order you like.

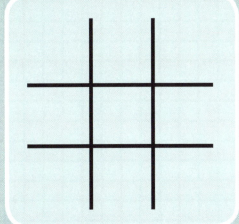

ABC	DEF	GHI
JKL	MNO	PQR
STU	VWX	YZ

Now, let's say you wanted to send the word: HELP

You would make up the symbol for each letter using the outline of the box and the number of the word.

So **"H"** is in the box shaped like this, ⌐ and it's the second letter. So the symbol for **"H"** is: ⌐2

"E" is the second letter in the box with this outline:⌐ So its symbol is this: ⌐2

L is this ⌐3

P is this ⌐1

So **HELP** looks like this: ⌐2 ⌐2 ⌐3 ⌐1

EXERCISE 3.3
"BUILD A PIGPEN"
HANDS-ON BOOK P.20
CREDITS: 20

LEARN TO USE A DICTIONARY CODE

Dictionary codes are excellent for hidden messages because without the right "key" book, they are extremely hard to crack.

Here's how you do it:

1. Find a dictionary, or a book with lots of words. This is your "key" book.

2. Write down your message in plain text.
   Let's use the message: **"My trousers are on fire."**
(Actually this would be a silly message to send via code. For one thing by the time the person you are writing to has read and deciphered the code, your trousers will be ruined.)

3. Look up the first word in your dictionary or key book.

4. Write down the page number, column number, line number and then word number of the word. In our example, the word "My" is on page 783, column 2, line 1, word 1 of my dictionary. So the code for "My" is: 783.2.1.1

5. Repeat this for the other words.
   Using my dictionary this results in:

783.2.1.1	1310.1.63.1	56.2.47.1	832.1.13.1	606.2.42.3
My	trousers	are	on	fire

Things to remember with this code:

1. The other person must be using EXACTLY the same book as you.

2. You must be very careful whilst counting. The slightest mistake makes a huge difference.
   For example, if I get two page numbers wrong, and write:

	783.2.1.1	1301.1.63.1	56.2.47.1	832.1.13.4	660.2.42.3
I get...	My	treasurer	is	in	Lapland

Which makes no sense whatsoever. (Unless your treasurer really has gone to Lapland. Although what your treasurer would be doing in Lapland is beyond me.)

You can make this code even harder by changing books. Say you have two books, make one "A" and one "B", each with their own system of counting. Then you could write, for example A783.2.1.1 B58, etc. This makes it even harder.

A SIMPLE NUMBER CIPHER

This code was invented by a Greek historian called Polybius, who lived from about 203-120 BC. He invented what is called the Polybius Square, a grid of 25 boxes into which each letter of the alphabet is put.

NUMBER CIPHERS

Here's how you do it:

1. Draw a 6 x 6 grid (six rows of six columns).

2. Put numbers and the letters of the alphabet in the grid. (You will notice you have to combine two letters. Y and Z are the best ones since they will be least used. For Polybius this wasn't a problem, since the Greek alphabet only had 24 letters.)

	1	2	3	4	5
1	A	B	C	D	E
2	F	G	H	I	J
3	K	L	M	N	O
4	P	Q	R	S	T
5	U	V	W	X	Y/Z

3. The code number for each letter is created by taking the row number and then the column number. So "A" is 11; "B" is 12; "M" is 33, etc. All the receiver has to do is use the same grid to decipher the letters.

CLASSIFIED: TOP SECRET

MEMOVSKI
Classified: Privateski
To: Head of Kaftanistan Secret Service
From: Even Colder Tibetan Office
Re: Loss of Code Book

Honoured Comrade, I am at loss to explain latest disaster, but I beg to report ultra-secret code book has gone missing from its secret hiding place (i.e. behind the portrait of Glorious Leader at opening of new Hydro-electric Post Office and Swimming Baths). On Wednesday we received visit from Tibetan rug salesman who spread out rug on floor. At all times, rug salesman was monitored, yet when he left the code book had gone. How could this be? It is mystery. Unless the rug somehow came to life and stole code book! I await news of my punishment and, no doubt, posting to Totally Freezing Vladivostok Office. In meantime we continue searching for rug salesman and his unusual rug with tassels shaped like four paws.

EXERCISE 3.4
"CREATE A NUMBER CIPHER"
HANDS-ON BOOK P.21
CREDITS: 10

CIPHERS

MASTERING CIPHERS

The use of ciphers goes back a long way. The Roman emperor, Julius Caesar, was skilled in their use. That's why one of the simplest ciphers is known as a "Caesar shift". In this, you create an alternative alphabet, where all the letters are shifted along.

Here's an example, where the letters have been shifted by three:

Plain text alphabet:	A B C D E F G H I J K L M N O P Q R S T U V W X Y Z
Cipher alphabet:	X Y Z A B C D E F G H I J K L M N O P Q R S T U V W

All you have to do is look for the letter you're using in the top row, and use the one in the row underneath it. Using this cipher, we can convert

this message: **BINKY IS A GOOD DOG**
Into this: **YFKHV FP X DLLA ALD**

We can make this more difficult to crack by taking the spaces out.
Which leaves: **YFKHVFPXDLLAALD**

The receiver of this message will only need to know the distance you have "shifted" the letters. However, this isn't very secure. If you wanted to crack a simple substitution code like this, all you'd have to do is try out the different alphabets until you found one that worked. So let's try a more difficult approach. In this one, you use a key phrase or a name. Instead of the alphabet, let's use something like, "The zebra will examine a skateboard in August".

First, we need to take out any repeated letters from our key phrase.
That leaves us with: **THEZBRAWILXMNSKODUG**
Then we need to add in the letters of the alphabet we haven't got.
In this case: **CFJPQVY**

So, our key becomes: **THEZBRAWILXMNSKODUGCFJPQVY**
Put that under the ordinary alphabet and you get the following:

Plain text alphabet:	A B C D E F G H I J K L M N O P Q R S T U V W X Y Z
Cipher alphabet:	T H E Z B R A W I L X M N S K O D U G C F J P Q V Y

Using this cipher, we can convert "Binky is a good dog" into:
HISXVIGTAKKZZKA

Even if a code breaker realises that this is a substitution, without the key, it's very hard to crack!

THE CIPHER DISC

The cipher disc provides an easy way of obtaining a substitution cipher. It was invented by Leon Battista Alberti in 1467. Alberti was a famous Italian philosopher and architect. He put two different alphabets on concentric rings (one ring is inside of or on top of another). To make a code, all you had to do was line up two different letters.

USING YOUR CIPHER DISC

All Spy School students are issued with instructions on how to make their own cipher disc. To find out how, please refer to p.22 of the hands-on book. Once you have made your disc, here's how to use it:

1. First, decide on the message you want to send.
2. Line up the "A" of the outer ring with a different letter on the inner ring.
3. Encrypt your message by substituting the letter on the inner ring for the one on the outer ring.
4. All the receiver has to do is line up the wheel in the same way as you have done.

CIPHER WHEEL

The cipher wheel is a more complex version of the disc. This is a kind of 3-D version, with many wooden discs of the same size mounted on an iron rod. The side of each disc has a scrambled alphabet written on it and is spun independently of the other wheels. To encode a message, the cryptographer would arrange the wheels so that one row spelt the message they wanted to send. Then they would simply copy down the letters from a different horizontal row on the wheel, write those letters down and send it to their receiver. To decipher the message, all the receiver had to do was arrange the wheels so that they matched the message they received.

EXERCISE 3.5
"CIPHER DISC"
HANDS-ON BOOK P.22
CREDITS: 10

TRANSPOSITION CIPHERS

A transposition cipher is when the letters of your message are moved around in a different pattern, rather than replaced by other letters.

For an example of a transposition, let's imagine you want to send the message:

MEET ME AFTER CLASS AND BRING THE PORCUPINE.

1. First you write the words in SIX columns
2. You then read the grid horizontally:

MALDTCEFABHUETSREPTESIPIMRANONECNGRE

And that's your enciphered message.
The receiver takes this message and writes it
in six parts horizontally:

M	A	L	D	T	C
E	F	A	B	H	U
E	T	S	R	E	P
T	E	S	I	P	I
M	R	A	N	O	N
E	C	N	G	R	E

MALDTC
EFABHU
ETSREP
TESIPI
MRANON
ECNGRE

VERTICAL ROUTE

Then they read it vertically, top to bottom. Sadly, this isn't hard to crack, since the code breaker will just try splitting the words into rows of different lengths, until he gets some words in columns that make sense. One of the ways round this is to do the transposition twice. In other words, take the phrase:

MALDTCEFABHUETSREPTESIPIMRANONECNGRE

and put it through another transposition.
This is twice as tricky to decipher!

Another way to make your transposition code harder to crack is to alter the route – that is the direction in which you write out the words. In our example we wrote our message running down, from the top of each column. But you could write it across, in a spiral, travelling in the other direction, etc. As long as the person receiving the message knows the direction you use!

CODES IN DIFFERENT DIRECTIONS

M	E	E	T	M	E
A	F	T	E	R	C
L	A	S	S	A	N
D	B	R	I	N	G
T	H	E	P	O	R
C	U	P	I	N	E

SIDE TO SIDE ROUTE

M	E	E	T	M	E
B	R	I	N	G	A
D	U	P	I	T	F
N	C	E	N	H	T
A	R	O	P	E	E
S	S	A	L	C	R

SPIRAL ROUTE

Another way to make transposition codes more complicated is to use a keyword. The keyword can be any word, as long as no letter is repeated in it. Let's use the word **MARKET**

What you do is this:

1. Write the keyword across the top of your columns.

2. Write the message using the route that you choose.

3. Encode your message by reading the new coded words in vertical lines, in alphabetical order of the keyword. So, in our example, you would start with the column under the "A" of "Market", then the column under "E", then "K", etc. The finished message would be:

EFABHU MRANON TESIPI MALDTC ETSREP ECNGRE

M	A	R	K	E	T
M	E	E	T	M	E
A	F	T	E	R	C
L	A	S	S	A	N
D	B	R	I	N	G
T	H	E	P	O	R
C	U	P	I	N	E

EXERCISE 3.6
"TRANSPOSITION CIPHER"
HANDS-ON BOOK P.23
CREDITS: 20

CRACKING THE CODE

It's one thing making codes: but what if you are presented with a code or a cipher that you have to crack?

Ciphers are easier to crack than codes. Solving a coded message is like trying to understand another language entirely. Without the "dictionary" it's very hard to crack. Unlike ciphers, codes don't necessarily have a logical pattern to them. However, the fact that you have to have a code book is also a potential weakness. Just think, it takes a lot of effort to make and distribute a code book. You have to think up the words, get the book printed then distribute it to your whole spy network. This means that the same code book might be used for months (or even years) before it is changed. During this period the enemy code breakers will be able to gather clues that enable them to reconstruct the code book, or they might even be able to steal a copy of the code book.

One method that code breakers use to crack a code is to look for repeated words. In English some words are more common than others, such as "the" or "and". Or they might look for places where the coded sentence seems to end: at least that will give them some kind of structure.

If you can collect lots of messages sent with the same code, that builds up your knowledge of the code language. And if you use further intelligence to match the message to certain events, or places or people, you might be able to figure out what is happening.

For example, let's say you get three messages about a place code-named "Lisbon". If, after these messages there is a break-in at the Spy HQ, you might deduce that "Lisbon" stands for "HQ".

In fact, the simplest way of cracking a code is often to steal the code book. This can be done through bribery, burglary, or raiding parties. This is the weak point of codes: lots of people need to have access to the code book. The more people who know the secret, the harder it is to keep.

Of course, what you want is for the enemy not to realise that you've got their code book. If they don't know you've got the code book, they'll carry on using it: and all the time you'll know what they're saying.

AGENT X SAYS,
"IT'S ONE THING CRACKING THE ENEMY CODE; THE PROBLEM COMES WHEN YOU HAVE TO CRACK YOUR OWN CODE! YOU REMEMBER HOW I LOST THE PLANS FOR THE ROCKET BASE? WELL I FOUND A MESSAGE THAT IS SUPPOSED TO GIVE ME A CLUE ABOUT THE LOCATION. BUT I CAN'T REMEMBER THE CIPHER KEY. IT SEEMS TO USE DIFFERENT CIPHERS. ANY IDEAS? HERE IT IS:"

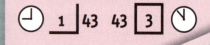

CRACKING A CIPHER

The strength of ciphers, as we have seen, is that they do not need a code book. They just need people to recognise the patterns. However, the fact that there is a pattern to most ciphers is also a sign of weakness. Because it makes them vulnerable to something called frequency analysis.

GET CRACKING

To illustrate this, let me tell you a story. Mary Queen of Scots was a rival of Elizabeth I for the throne of England. Elizabeth had Mary put into prison, and while she was there, Mary used a secret cipher to send messages to her conspirators – messages that plotted to kill Elizabeth. She used a symbol cipher, with symbols substituted for letters. This code became known as the Babington Cipher, because Mary sent it to her former page, Anthony Babington. Sadly (for Mary at least), Queen Elizabeth's spies intercepted her messages and set to work on breaking the cipher.

They were able to do this because every letter in a language appears with a certain average frequency. In English, for example, "E" appears much more frequently than "Z". "E" is the most common letter, followed by "T" and then "A". The most commonly occurring pair of letters is "TH". So, if you are faced with a cipher, what you look for first is the most frequent symbol. When you've found that, you try matching it with the most frequent letter.

If there are lots of "G's" for example, that might be a substitution for "E". Elizabeth's code breakers used frequency analysis to decipher the letters of Mary Queen of Scots. Mary and her collaborators were found guilty of treason and executed in 1587.

Nowadays, code breakers use powerful computers to decrypt ciphers. These computers run decryption software, which looks for patterns and can do millions of different calculations on encrypted messages. However, just as the decryption programmes have got more powerful, so have the encryption programmes. Some codes generated by computers are incredibly hard to crack. So today, there is more emphasis on other ways of finding out – like bugging and surveillance.

"THE EARLIEST KNOWN DESCRIPTION OF THE TECHNIQUE OF FREQUENCY ANALYSIS WAS WRITTEN IN THE 9TH CENTURY AD (THAT'S OVER A THOUSAND YEARS AGO) BY AN ARAB SCIENTIST WITH AN INCREDIBLY LONG NAME: ABU YUSUF YA 'QUB IBN IS-HAQ IBN AS-SABBAH IBN 'OMRAN IBN ISMAIL AL-KINDI. AL-KINDI, AS HE WAS KNOWN FOR SHORT, WROTE NEARLY 300 BOOKS ON MEDICINE, ASTRONOMY, MATHEMATICS AND MUSIC, BUT HIS MOST FAMOUS WORK IS CALLED A MANUSCRIPT ON DECIPHERING CRYPTOGRAPHIC MESSAGES. IT WAS ONLY REDISCOVERED IN 1987 IN A LIBRARY IN ISTANBUL."

INVISIBLE INK

MAKE YOUR OWN INVISIBLE INK!

Picture this scenario: you have to leave a message urgently, but you don't have a code book handy. How will you write your message down so that nobody can find it?

Invisible ink - that's how!

And you don't need expensive supplies. No, all the resourceful spy needs for very basic, quick invisible writing is a lemon. Yes, that's all.

Here's what you do:

1. Squeeze the lemon into a cup.

2. Use an old fashioned fountain pen nib to write with lemon juice. Or you can simply dip your finger in and write with that.

3. As the lemon juice dries it will fade and disappear from view.

4. All you have to do to bring it back is put the piece of paper on a warm radiator. As the paper warms up the writing will reappear.

This is not a sophisticated system, but it will work.

AGENT X SAYS, "YOU CAN ALSO USE YOUR OWN URINE, BUT, FRANKLY, IT'S TOUGH ENOUGH BEING A SPY WITHOUT RESORTING TO THAT."

OTHER FORMS OF INVISIBLE WRITING

If you have access to a candle, you can make a wax pencil. Take a bit of wax and rub it between your hands until it warms. Form it into a thin pencil-like shape, then let it cool and harden slightly. You can then write on a piece of paper. The words will be invisible until your contact uses a wash of water colour. Alternatively they can sprinkle the sheet with chalk dust which will stick to the wax, but shake off the rest of the paper.

QXTL3 GG569 SAYS, "WELL DONE! OR TO PUT IT ANOTHER WAY, 53 15 32 32 14 35 34 15. YOU HAVE MADE YOUR WAY THROUGH THE MAZE OF CODES AND CIPHERS. NOW GO ON FROM HERE TO MAKE EVER MORE FIENDISHLY DIFFICULT SECRET MESSAGES. AND REMEMBER: NEVER LOSE YOUR CODE BOOK!"

USING YOUR SPY PEN

You can also write secret messages using the spy pen in this pack. Write an invisible message with one end of the pen. Then use the other pen to reveal it.

GADGETS AND EQUIPMENT

Now, pay attention. In this section, we'll be looking at some spy gadgets that are very complicated, delicate and expensive. So don't touch anything. And don't press any buttons. And put out of your head all that movie nonsense of flying cars, exploding wristwatches and pens that double as rocket launchers. We boffins in espionage development and research have better things to do than dream up outlandish devices or highly improbable vehicles. Subterfuge and cunning is a better way to operate than stealing a tank and blowing the door down. Good observation skills and a quick brain are key. Remember, these gadgets are only as good as the person using them, so please take care. Especially with the ones that go boom. Whether or not they're disguised as a wristwatch.

Prof. James Rimmington, "R".

IN THIS SECTION

1. SPY CAMERAS
2. GADGETS TO HELP YOU HEAR
3. GADGETS TO HELP YOU ON THE PHONE
4. COUNTER-SURVEILLANCE GADGETS
5. GADGETS TO HELP YOU SEE
6. TRAVEL AND TRANSPORT
7. UNARMED COMBAT
8. HIDING PLACES

SPY CAMERAS

Miniature cameras have been used for many years by spies. Some were designed to photograph documents, others to take photos of people and buildings, and a special type of camera was used for the copying of miniaturised photographic images via microdots. Today, digital technology means that miniature cameras can take video as well as still photographs.

TAKE PICTURES WITHOUT BEING SEEN

One way is not to conceal the camera at all. Instead you can make it look like you're not using it. The camera sits on the table, with its lens cap firmly on. The spy operates it using a hidden shutter release, and the lens cap has tiny holes in it, through which a photo can be taken. Another way is to use a dummy lens, with the real lens pointing sideways at a 90-degree angle. The operator, disguised perhaps as a tourist, takes a photo in one direction, when he's actually pointing his lens in a different direction entirely!

This lens is a dummy. It just points straight ahead.

The real lens, hidden inside, uses mirrors to point at a 90-degree angle.

Perhaps the most famous spy camera ever was the Minox subminiature camera, which for its size, produced exceptionally good photographs. Naturally, miniature cameras don't have the features you'd expect of a normal camera: often you don't have a viewfinder. All spies, therefore, have to practise so they know when an image is in view without being able to see it through the lens.

AGENT X SAYS, "SPIES HAVE USED TRAINED ANIMALS TO TAKE PHOTOS. IN THE PAST, CAMERAS HAVE BEEN STRAPPED TO TRAINED PIGEONS. THEY DID ONCE TRY TO TRAIN BINKY TO TAKE PHOTOS, BUT ALL THEY GOT WAS SOME GRASS, HIS FOOD BOWL AND SOME PICTURES OF OTHER DOGS FROM RATHER HORRIBLE ANGLES."

MICRODOT CAMERAS

In the 1950s and 1960s, scientists developed microdot cameras where the image was reduced to the size of a tiny dot. Microdots were ideal for passing messages because they could easily be hidden in other messages – as the dot on the top of the letter "i", for example. To view the images, you needed to magnify them many times.

One spy organisation produced an ingenious microdot viewer that was hidden in a fountain pen.

HIDDEN SURVEILLANCE CAMERAS

Surveillance cameras can be hidden in a wide variety of disguises. The better types are wireless, meaning there are no cables to worry about. They can transmit live video up to 228 m (750 ft) away.

- You can wear them – such as in a baseball cap, or concealed behind sunglasses.
- You can put them into a watch or into the packet of sweets you have on the table of the cafe.
- You can put them into some other portable objects, like a briefcase, or the radio in the picture below. (The camera is hidden behind the front of the unit.) All you have to do is point it in the right direction and attach a linked receiver to a VCR or TV.

EVEN SMALLER HIDDEN CAMERAS

All these devices are possible because cameras are now so small. One camera, for example, is less than 8.5 mm square ($1/3$-inch square) and requires only a 1.5 mm ($1/16$-inch) hole to look through. This means that you can hide wireless surveillance cameras almost anywhere. They can be hidden in wall clocks or smoke alarms, or even, as in this case, a tiny screw. The pinhole lens peeps out from the top of the screw, recording all that is going on.

Beware! Even your flatpack furniture could be watching you!

EXERCISE 4.1
"WHO'S WATCHING YOU?"
HANDS-ON BOOK P.26
CREDITS: 18

GADGETS TO HELP YOU HEAR

DISGUISED MICROPHONES

Just as there are many ways to hide a camera, there are many ways to hide a microphone. There are two types of microphone: wired, where a concealed wire runs to an even more concealed tape recorder; and wireless, where the microphone transmits the signal . . . er . . . without wires. Microphones can be hidden in pens, or clipped behind clothing like ties, jackets, etc.

DIGITAL VOICE RECORDER / MP3 PLAYER

A digital voice recorder, or MP3 player is a handy gadget: it can store many hours of audio, which can be downloaded to a computer. You can also connect it to mobile phones to record phone calls. Some come with alarm clocks to allow conversations to be recorded automatically at certain times. And when there's nothing else happening, you can play your music on it.

WATCH VOICE RECORDER

Voice recorders can be disguised as well. Here's one disguised in a watch, with 256MB flash memory built in. It allows you to record up to 9 hours of voice recording, which can be downloaded to your computer.

DISTANCE MICROPHONES

Miniature microphones are all very well, but you have to be close to your subject. What if they're over the other side of the street? If you are in a suitably hidden position, you might get away with using a sound amplifier. This can magnify faint or distant sounds. The microphone picks up the sounds, which are then passed through an amplifier to headphones. The conversation can also be recorded. Of course, you have to be well hidden to use one of these, since you have to be able to point it at your quarry.

THE SPY MOUSE

Microphones can even be hidden in a computer mouse. A spy mouse can pick up telephone conversations, discussions, phone tones that have been dialled, etc. And all the time the user thinks it's just a mouse . . .

GADGETS TO HELP YOU ON THE PHONE

HELPING YOU HEAR

VOICE CHANGER

A telephone voice changer is a gadget that straps to the mouthpiece of your phone. By adjusting a switch your voice can be instantly disguised. You can get models that strap onto the mouthpiece of the phone, or that plug into the telephone socket (you then plug your phone line into the box).

TELEPHONE TONE DECODER

You know how telephone keys make different tones? A tone decoder listens to the tones that a phone has dialled and displays the numbers on a screen. You don't need to have it connected to the phone, you can play a recording of what was dialled and it will display the numbers.

PHONE RECORDERS

This box connects to the phone and records all the phone calls made, along with the time and the date. It automatically starts when the receiver is lifted, and stops when the phone is replaced. However, given that it's quite a big box, it's not much good for covert surveillance. It's probably better for recording calls made to you, rather than calls being made by someone else.

CLASSIFIED: TOP SECRET

MEMOROV

Classified: Nopeepski

To: Head of Kaftanistan Secret Service
From: Totally Freezing Vladivostok Office
Re: Failure of Surveillance

Honoured Comrade, we have had some problems with the surveillance. As you ordered, we hid many microphones in suspect's hotel room, in places such as alarm clock, mirror, lampstand and in the nose of statue of Glorious Leader Looking Heroic. However, when playing back recordings, instead of location of secret rocket plans, all we heard was a lot of barking, and man shouting, "Get down Binky, it's not a real parrot." We tried to arrest suspect, but he left disguised as Pirate during Vladivostok's Annual Freezing Cold Carnival Parade. Given I have failed again, I have decided to do honourable thing and run away. Having helped myself to contents of your personal bank account, I will spend rest of my days on very warm Caribbean beach.

EXERCISE 4.2
"COUNTER-SURVEILLANCE QUIZ"
SEE P.55 OF YOUR MANUAL FOR MORE INFORMATION

COUNTER-SURVEILLANCE GADGETS

Using special equipment is all very well, but how do you know if someone is using the same stuff on you? How do you make sure that you are not being recorded or filmed? More gadgets of course! There are gadgets to help you remain secure from eavesdroppers or snoopers.

BUG DETECTOR

This is a vital piece of kit. A small, handheld box, it can scan the room, detecting hidden microphones, transmitters and cameras. One sweep of this and you can be sure that your room is pretty secure. Although it won't tell you if the person you are talking to is really on your side or not . . .

PHONE TAP DETECTOR

Worried that your phone conversations are being recorded? This little device checks your phone line is behaving itself. It will indicate whether the line has been tampered with and whether somebody else is beginning to listen, the minute you pick up the phone.

VIDEO-CAMERA DETECTOR

This brilliant device not only detects the presence of a hidden video camera, it can also show you what it's filming! You'll be able to pick up exactly what the camera is seeing, making it easy to discover the hidden device.

WHITE-NOISE GENERATOR

If you can't find them, deafen them. This machine generates a blanket of white noise around the perimeter of the room. (White noise sounds like a load of hissing, like the sound you get when a radio isn't tuned in properly.) The sound cannot be filtered out, meaning that whatever listening devices are in your room, and wherever they're hidden, your conversation will remain private.

AGENT X SAYS, "ALWAYS REMEMBER THAT IF YOU HAVE A GREAT GADGET, AN ENEMY SPY MAY HAVE A BETTER ONE. IF YOU HAVE A PEN THAT ACTS AS A RADIO RECEIVER, STUN GUN AND CAMERA, THEY MIGHT HAVE ONE THAT ACTS AS A RADIO RECEIVER, STUN GUN AND CAMERA, AND ALSO DOES THE WASHING UP. OR EVEN GOES "BOING". WHAT MAKES YOU A BETTER SPY THAN THEM IS NOT YOUR GADGETS BUT YOUR BRAIN."

GADGETS TO HELP YOU SEE

PEEPHOLE REVERSER

You know those peepholes people have in their front doors? Well this device lets you "peep" on them. Simply place it over the peephole and you can look into the house, hallway or room, assessing any potential threats waiting for you behind the door. You can also get video cameras that work the other way; they mount in place of an ordinary door peephole, allowing you to see who's there on a TV or video monitor. That way you don't even have to go to the door.

NIGHT-VISION GOGGLES

For the spy, darkness is a friend. Although it's less of a friend if you end up bumping into things and shouting, "Ouch, my foot!" That's where these goggles come in. Night-vision goggles use image intensifiying technology to convert weak light from the visible and near-infrared spectrum to visible light. (Which roughly translated means that you can see in the dark.) Make sure it is dark, though, as anyone seeing you wearing these will suspect that you are up to something.

COMPACT BINOCULARS

A pair of compact binoculars are a basic tool of the spy's trade. Look for ones that are small, light and that fit into your pocket. Or you can use a mini spy-scope. These weigh 30-50 g (1 - 1.5 oz) and are just over 5 cm (2 in) long – they can also be used as a microscope. And if there are no spies around, you can always go birdwatching.

EXERCISE 4.2
"COUNTER-SURVEILLANCE QUIZ"
HANDS-ON BOOK P.27
CREDITS: 10

FLEXIBLE-FIBRE CAMERAS

For those of you who want a more versatile camera, flexible-fibre cameras can slide under doors and through grilles, or gaps in the wall. They are good for assessing danger, since you can use them from a distance.

TRAVEL AND TRANSPORT

Here's what often happens when young would-be spies enter my laboratory. They look around at all the gadgets, all the bug detectors and voice recorders and then they ask, "Where's the car?" What they mean is the very flash sports car from the films, the one that turns into a submarine/jetplane/three-bedroomed house with swimming pool and garage. Real spies do not use such things.

CARS

There are times when a special vehicle would be useful.
A bullet-proof car, for example, is built to withstand small attacks.

Passenger compartment protected by lightweight armour plating, protects against hand guns and submachine guns.

Bullet-proof glass on all windows, with front armoured windscreen as well.

High security dead-bolt system to each door

Automatic and manual under-bonnet fire extinguisher system

Full radiator Protection

Undercar armour plating to protect against bombs, etc.

Ballistic steel and nylon flat tyre inserts means that the car can still drive with punctured tyres.

AGENT X SAYS, "REAL SPIES ARE NOT SHOW-OFFS. ANY STUDENT WHO ARRIVES AT SPY SCHOOL DRIVING AN ASTON MARTIN OR A FERRARI WILL BE DOCKED 50 CREDITS. NO PROFESSIONAL SPY DRIVES A FLASHY CAR. INSTEAD, YOU MUST DRIVE WHAT EVERYONE ELSE DRIVES. OR BETTER STILL USE THE BUS. THAT WAY YOU CAN STEAL STATE SECRETS AND REDUCE CARBON EMISSIONS AT THE SAME TIME."

GPS TRACKING DEVICES

GPS (Global positioning system) tracking devices use satellite signals to track a vehicle's location, speed and direction.

EXERCISE 4.3
"DESIGN A SPY VEHICLE"
HANDS-ON BOOK P.28
CREDITS: 10

UNARMED COMBAT

A lot of would-be spies visit my department and all they want to do is talk about guns. Nasty, noisy things. No, far better is to travel light and learn how to defend yourself without having to resort to extreme measures.

NINJA SPIES

At the Amazing Academy School of Spying and Espionage we specialise in Ninja techniques. The Ninjas, often thought of as the world's first special forces, originated in Japan in the 15th century. A typical Ninja assignment would be stealing sensitive documents, or mapping an enemy's castle in preparation for a siege. Typical spy work, in fact. Along with special combat skills, they use a range of Ninja equipment including handclaws (to climb walls and roofs), small tubes to listen through walls and even smoke grenades to help their escape.

AGENT X SAYS, "YOU WILL NOTE THAT THERE IS NO USE OF GUNS OR WEAPONS ALLOWED AT THE SCHOOL OF SPYING AND ESPIONAGE. SPYING IS DANGEROUS ENOUGH WITHOUT CARRYING AROUND SOMETHING THAT MIGHT GO "BANG!" AT ANY MOMENT. ANYWAY, REALLY WELL TRAINED ASSASSINS DON'T NEED A GUN. THEY CAN KILL PEOPLE WITH WHATEVER THEY FIND. I KNEW ONE SPY WHO COULD DEFEND HIMSELF WITH A VERY SHARP CROISSANT."

STUN PEN

This stun pen is the size of a highlighter pen, but it delivers a shock of 500,000 volts. Use this and your enemy will quickly become dazed and drop to the ground. He won't be dead, and you can still make your escape.

HIDING PLACES

Every spy needs a place to hide secrets (usually secrets they have stolen from other hiding places). Here are a few gadgets that will help you to hide your confidential information.

DIVERSION SAFES

These look like ordinary household items, but they have secret compartments. You can get safes shaped like cans of drink – just put them in the refrigerator and no-one will be able to tell the difference. Other diversion safes can look like electric plug sockets, books, or even rocks.

HIDDEN DEVICES

If you have to carry something around with you – a microfilm for example – then a hollow coin is useful. If necessary, you can drop it into a wishing well or a fountain if you are being followed. In the past, film was hidden in things like fake batteries, tins of shaving cream, even in a fake eyeball. Some devices had a special way of opening: if anyone opened them the wrong way, a burst of acid would destroy the contents.

AGENT X SAYS, "I USED TO HAVE A SPECIALLY MADE PAIR OF SHOES WITH A HIDING PLACE UNDER THE SOLE TO CONCEAL MESSAGES. THIS WAS A VERY GOOD PLACE TO HIDE THINGS SINCE THE SMELL OF MY FEET PUT PEOPLE OFF INVESTIGATING FURTHER. I HAVE ALSO USED HIDDEN COMPARTMENTS IN SUITCASES, BOOKS AND EVEN FAKE BIRDS SUCH AS PIGEONS AND PARROTS. WHICH REMINDS ME, WHERE DID I PUT THOSE PLANS?"

"R" SAYS, "WELL DONE. YOU'VE PAID ATTENTION TO ALL I'VE SAID AND HAVE SUCCESSFULLY COMPLETED THIS PART OF YOUR COURSE. I TRUST THAT YOU WILL GO ON FROM HERE TO USE (AND INVENT) MANY NEW GADGETS TO HELP YOU IN YOUR LIFE OF ESPIONAGE!"

EXERCISE 4.4
"CREATE A HOLLOW BOOK"
HANDS-ON BOOK P.29
CREDITS: 20

ADDITIONAL INFORMATION

IN THIS SECTION . . .

SPECIAL COURSES

GUEST LECTURES

ANNUAL BANQUET AND AWARDS CEREMONY

THE SPY SHOP

SCHOOL OF SPYING CLUBS AND SOCIETIES

IMPORTANT
THE SECRET ENTRANCE IN THE LIBRARY WILL BE OUT OF USE FOR THREE DAYS FOR MAINTENANCE. DURING THAT TIME USE THE ALTERNATIVE ENTRANCE, IN THE HOLLOW OAK TREE BY THE DUCK POND.

LOST!
ONE SET OF ROCKET INSTALLATION PLANS.

IF FOUND PLEASE CONTACT AGENT X.

NOTICE
THE CODE BREAKING CLUB WILL MEET IN THE FF556D00 AT KKJHO5663. (IF YOU CAN'T CRACK THIS, YOU CAN'T COME!)

STOP!
PLEASE DO NOT USE THE STAFF PHOTOGRAPHS TO PRACTISE YOUR DISGUISES.

EXTRAS

SPECIAL COURSES

In addition to the basic course offered here, students at the Academy can sign up for a number of additional courses that might be of interest. Some of these are run in conjunction with other Amazing Academy schools.

SPECIAL PRIZE
HAVE YOU WORKED OUT WHERE AGENT X HID THE SECRET PLANS? THERE ARE CLUES THROUGHOUT THIS MANUAL. (TRY LOOKING AT THE MEMOS FROM KAFTANISTAN AS WELL.) THERE WILL BE A SPECIAL AWARD OF 50 CREDITS IF YOU GET IT RIGHT! YOU CAN FIND THE ANSWER IN YOUR HANDS-ON BOOK ON P.31.

STUDY WEEK: UNDERWATER ESPIONAGE

Led by Agent X, with equipment from the Spy School laboratory, this is a chance for some handpicked students to spend a week getting wet. In conjunction with the Amazing Academy School of Underwater Adventure, we will be learning: underwater sabotage techniques, how to operate mini-submarines and how to set underwater explosives.
Bring a towel.

"BUGGING" WEEK

During the summer term we will be having our annual competition to see which student can bug the most offices around the Amazing Academy campus. As normal, double points will be scored for anyone who can bug the office of the Dean. And triple points for anyone who can bug the office of Agent X.

SHORT COURSE: LIVING AS SOMEONE ELSE

This is a four-day, intensive course where you can wander around the Amazing Academy campus pretending to be someone else. You'll start off by creating your character, then spend three days living the life of your creation. Special credits will be awarded for anyone who manages to set up an account under their assumed name at the Amazing Academy Bank.

GUEST LECTURES

During the year we will have a series of guest lectures by distinguished spies and secret agents. Forthcoming lectures will include:

Agent X: Tails of Espionage: How one spy and his dog infiltrated top-secret installations, stole confidential plans and still had time for walkies.

Anonymous: Secrets of the Kaftanistani Secret Service
(Live videocast from a beach somewhere in the Caribbean)

The Joy of Disguises: A special lecture by Madame LeFarge, during which she will transform herself around 73 times. Students are invited to come in disguise. No pirates admitted.

Code name "Raven": The History of the Black Chambers
The code master known only as Raven is one of the most respected cryptographers in the world of espionage. This lecture on the history of codes and ciphers will be delivered entirely in a code language of Raven's own making. Students are recommended to record the lecture and then spend several weeks trying to work out what it was he was actually saying.

ANNUAL BANQUET AND AWARDS CEREMONY

The School of Spying and Espionage Annual Banquet and Awards Ceremony is a highlight of the year. (The banquet, actually, is held elsewhere, since we usually challenge ourselves to take on alternative identities and infiltrate somebody else's end of term banquet.)

The awards cover the following categories:

- Best disguise
- Best tracker
- Best spy
- Student who has created most convincing false identity
- Best student-invented gadget
- Spy Student of the Year
- Winner of the "Bug Agent X's Office" Competition

Last year's "Spy Student of the Year" is presented with his prize by Agent X.

AMAZING ACADEMY SPY SHOP

All these goods – and many more – are available in the Spy Shop on the upper floor of the department. You can also find an extensive range of books, clothing, gadgets, the ideal Christmas gift for the special spy in your life, etc. in the main Amazing Academy Campus Store.

Drab colours mean you can blend into most backgrounds.

CLOTHES

THE SCHOOL OF SPYING AND ESPIONAGE SURVEILLANCE COAT

Specially created by our tutors, this coat comes with a range of features suitable for all surveillance environments.

- Reversible material, so you can change its colour.
- Built-in pockets for gadgets, disguises, etc.
- Optional thermal lining to keep you warm on those remote polar satellite bases.
- Pre-wired for headphones, etc.
- Available in a range of very boring, drab and instantly forgettable colours.

EQUIPMENT

THE MULTI-PURPOSE BASIC FACIAL HAIR

This artificial facial hair has been specially designed to provide spies with a quick change. You can shape it into moustaches, beards, sideburns, eyebrows, etc. Or even put it on your chest to make you more manly.

THE RIMMINGTON MICRO CAMERA

This digital micro camera is small enough to fit in your pocket, but still capable of taking holiday snaps. The camera includes a GPS tracker and wireless microphone. It comes in a range of disguise styles including matchbox, wristwatch and donut.

Deluxe models also include a mini TV screen so you can watch movies when you're bored.

■ BOOKS

We stock a wide selection of books. Some of our bestsellers include:

THE SCHOOL CODE BOOKS

Offering a wide range of codes and ciphers, this is the book for those who want to get even more cryptic. It covers all the basics, but also includes the more complicated "Binky" code, where every word is translated into dog language. (Warning: if you're going to master this code, you'll need to be able to bark. Not to mention sniff your own bottom.)

NOW PAY ATTENTION, MY LIFE IN GADGETS BY "R"

A wonderful, although some would say rather too detailed, look at exactly how spy gadgets work. With lots of diagrams.

MY LIFE AS AN UNDERCOVER LIBRARIAN BY AGENT X

A limited edition book showing how Agent X travelled the world, stealing secrets, while pretending to be a librarian.

MY LIFE AS AN UNDERCOVER LIBRARIAN'S WIFE BY MRS X

A rather surprising book showing how she knew about Agent X all along, and was actually working for the same people.

■ TRANSPORT

SPY SKATES

Due to customer demand for inconspicuous transport packed with high-tech gizmos, we have developed Spy Skates.

Spy Skates offer the perfect solution to high-speed tracking. For extra-fast pursuits, there is a jet pack option available.

The skates also come with the following add-ons:

- Cameras fitted into the back allowing you to film your quarry.
- GPS transmitter linked to a hidden earpiece for accurate positioning and navigation.
- Distance microphone disguised in wheel.

IF YOU ARE INTERESTED IN JOINING ANY MORE AMAZING ACADEMY COURSES, PLEASE VISIT WWW.AMAZING-ACADEMY.COM TO FIND OUT MORE!

EXTRAS

CLUBS AND SOCIETIES

The School of Spying and Espionage has many clubs and societies which may be of interest to you. Tick the boxes for those you would like to join.

☐ **QUICK CHANGE DISGUISE SOCIETY**

For anyone interested in developing rapid changes of appearance.
Where: Dressing up box, School of Spying and Espionage
When: Wednesdays 14.30

☐ **EXPLOSION CLUB**

This is a responsible society dedicated to the careful use of explosives, detonators, hidden charges, etc. That and we just love anything that goes boom.
Where: Normally in the lecture room, but at the moment we're meeting elsewhere while the lecture room is rebuilt.
When: Tuesdays 19.00

☐ **NINJA AND MARTIAL ARTS SOCIETY**

Learn a variety of martial arts including Kung Fu, Tae Kwon do, and Sudoko.
Where: Spy School Training Room
When: Fridays 18.00

☐ **THE BLACK CHAMBER**

For centuries, secret services around the world have run "Black Chambers" – secret rooms where the code makers and code breakers worked.
The term comes from France where, during the eighteenth century the Cabinet noir (French for "black room") was the room where letters of suspected persons were intercepted, opened and read by government spies, before being sent on to the location. Our Black Chamber is more fun: it's a club for anyone who wants to try their hands at more complicated codes and ciphers. On the whole we will not be intercepting anyone's letters or emails. Well, not unless they're really interesting.
Where: The Code Room
When: Wednesdays 20.00

AGENT X SAYS, "WELL DONE TO ALL OF YOU ON REACHING THE END OF THE COURSE.
NOW THE TASK IS TO TAKE WHAT YOU HAVE LEARNT AND USE IT FOR GOOD. OUR JOB AS SPIES IS TO FIGHT FOR FREEDOM, AND TO USE THE SKILLS WE HAVE TO MAKE THE WORLD A BETTER PLACE. SPYING IS A MURKY, DANGEROUS BUSINESS FULL OF DIFFICULT AND COMPLEX CHOICES. (SO IS BEING A LIBRARIAN, ACTUALLY.) SO STAY TRUE TO YOURSELF, MAKE YOUR OWN DECISIONS AND TRUST NO-ONE. EXCEPT, PERHAPS, YOUR POODLE."